NAVMC 2686

APPRENTICESHIP PROGRAM FOR MOS OF

AUTOMOTIVE MECHANIC

WORK EXPERIENCE LOG

APPRENTICE NAME

DEPARTMENT OF THE NAVY
HEADQUARTERS UNITED STATES MARINE CORPS
WASHINGTON, D.C. 20380

TABLE OF CONTENTS

INTRODUCTION

APPRENTICESHIP

Apprenticeship is training for jobs in technical trades that require special skills and knowledge. It involves technical schooling and planned on-the-job training under supervision. For young workers desiring to gain a skilled occupation, the apprenticeship program provides a step by step program of instruction and on-the-job training. This program will lead to advance standing in the technical skill or trade you have chosen.

The USMC Apprentice Program provides you with the opportunity to meet some requirements for advancement of your chosen skill area while on active duty. As you progress in your training in the Marine Corps and master the skills required of your trade, you will have the mastered skills recorded in your log. Your apprenticeship program allows you to make your work experience in the Marine Corps count twice. First, to fulfill your active duty obligation, in a productive manner. Second, to provide you with a usable skill if you should decide to return to civilian life. By having documented proof of Marine Corps schooling and work experience, you should qualify for a better job at higher pay.

Most apprenticeship terms range from 1 to 4 years, depending upon the trade involved. To master a particular trade requires: (1) Learning all or most of the skills of the trade; (2) Perfecting each specific skill; (3) Bringing each skill up to the speed and accuracy required of the job; and (4) Learning to use specific skills in combination with other skills.

MARINE CORPS APPRENTICESHIP PROGRAM

The purpose of establishing the Marine Corps Apprenticeship Program is to provide Marine Corps commanders an opportunity to implement programs of apprenticeship for military personnel in occupations closely related and applicable to private industry needs and requirements. Marine Corps school training and experience in the field will, if properly documented, satisfy private industry requirements for the training of apprentices in nationally recognized apprenticeable occupations.

The ultimate objective of the United States Marine Corps Apprenticeship Program is to provide registered certification of an individual Marine's skilled craft occupational training. The program has been designed to achieve recognition for Marines equal to their civilian counterparts.

Registration of the National Apprenticeship Standards for the United States Marine Corps with the Bureau of Apprenticeship and Training, U.S. Department of Labor, is beneficial to the Marine Corps, to individual Marines, and to private industry, management and labor. Acceptance of U.S. Marine Corps apprentices as skilled craft-workers by private industry, management and labor will enhance Marines' employment opportunities as veterans, shorten the term of private industry apprenticeship through the award of appropriate credit for previous military training experience, and provide a source of registered skilled personnel to meet national manpower requirements.

THE AUTOMOTIVE SERVICE MECHANIC APPRENTICESHIP PROGRAM

The purpose of this pamphlet is to announce the United States Marine Corps Apprenticeship Program for the trade of Automotive Service Mechanic.

Policies and procedures for participation in the program are contained in MCO 1550.22.

Marines holding a primary or secondary MOS indicated below and who are serving in that MOS may participate in the program.

     MOS 3521   Organizational Automotive Mechanic
     MOS 3522   Field Automotive Mechanic
     MOS 3529   Maintenance Chief
     MOS 3524   Fuel and Electrical Systems Repairperson

This is an 8000 hours program which leads to a certification of journeyman in the trade of Automotive Mechanic by the U.S. Department of Labor. Participation in the program is voluntary, and no membership in labor unions or professional associations is required. The work process schedule and schedule of related instruction are outlined in Appendixes A and B. The purpose of the work process schedule and the schedule of related instruction is as indicated below:

     The work process schedule reflects categories of work experience required by Marine apprentices to qualify as Journeyman Automotive Mechanics.

     The schedule of related instruction identifies courses which are available to Marine apprentices to satisfy the 144 hours of annual related instruction required for completion of the program.

Marines eligible for the program may enroll by contacting the Unit or Base Education Officer who will assist in the preparation of the application.

Apprentice logs and instructions on their use will be provided by the Education Officer at the time of registration. Marine apprentices will be required to maintain their log sheets on a daily basis. Log entries must be verified by the Marine apprentice's immediate supervisor on a weekly basis.

Marines who have partially completed an approved Federal or State registered civilian apprenticeship will be awarded credit within the constraints of the individual apprenticeship training program standards. Each training hour successfully completed in the occupation involved will be awarded credit upon presentation of authenticated documentation. Marines serving an enlistment beyond their initial enlistment, and therefore considered career Marines, may make application for the apprenticeship program in order to be certified as having completed an apprentice program. Career Marine apprentices must complete the same requirements as the first-term apprentice except that they will be given credit for one-half the hours required for the specific apprenticeship program in which they are enrolled provided their previous enlistment was served in an MOS applicable to the relevant apprenticeship program for which applying.

Organized related instruction for all United States Marine Corps apprentices will be defined by the individual apprenticeship program standards. Such related instruction will be provided on an hour-per-year basis, or the total hours may be achieved through the successful completion of a multiweek training course for the apprenticeable occupation involved at any United States Marine Corps training school, or other Service School (Army, Navy, etc.) providing such training.

Upon successful completion of apprenticeship training and experience requirements as prescribed by individual apprenticeship program standards, the apprentice will submit a request via the chain of command, accompanied by a letter from the appropriate commander or education officer, to the Office of National Industry Promotion, Bureau of Apprenticeship and Training, U.S. Department of Labor, Washington, D.C. 20213, for issuance of a Certificate of Completion of Apprenticeship (Enclosure 10). The Bureau of Apprenticeship and Training will issue all Certificates of Completion of Apprenticeship to the individual through Headquarters, U.S. Marine Corps (Code OTTE) to the appropriate commander.

NATIONAL APPRENTICESHIP STANDARDS

FOR

THE UNITED STATES MARINE CORPS

Developed by Headquarters, United States
Marine Corps, Washington, D.C., with the
assistance of the Bureau of Apprenticeship
and Training, Employment and Training
Administration, United States Department
of Labor, Washington, D. C.

AUTHORITY

National Apprenticeship Standards for the United States
Marine Corps are established by authority of:

_____
W. GRAHAM CLAYTOR JR.
Secretary of the Navy

_____
RAY MARSHALL
Secretary, United States
Department of Labor

_____
LOUIS H. WILSON
Commandant of the
Marine Corps

Registered as incorporating the basic standards
recommended by tile Bureau of Apprenticeship and
Training, Employment and Training Administration,
United States Department of Labor.

_____
HUGH C. MURPHY
Administrator
Bureau of Apprenticeship and Training
Employment and Training Administration

Registration Number N-91040   Date July 7, 1977

DEFINITIONS

1. EMPLOYER----------------------------The United States Marine Corps

2. PROGRAM SPONSOR--------------------Commanding Officer
    Motor Transport School Company
    Marine Corps Service Support
    Schools Marine Corps Base Camp
    Lejeune, North Carolina 28542

3. NATIONAL APPRENTICESHIP. STANDARDS - The entire document which
    embodies the procedures for the
    selection and training of Marine
    Corps apprentices and sets forth
    all the conditions associated
    therewith, including training on
    the job, related technical
    instruction, and administrative
    responsibilities.

4. WORK EXPERIENCE LOG-----------------A book issued to each registered
    apprentice identifying the
    occupation, work process training
    schedule, hours allocated to each
    training task increment in the
    work process schedule, and super-
    visory certification
    requirements.

5. APPRENTICE-------------------------Any individual who is on active
    duty in the U.S. Marine Corps,
    meets entry age requirements,
    performs assignments that include
    training in an apprenticeable
    occupation and who is registered
    with the Bureau of Apprenticeship
    and Training, U. S. Department
    of Labor, Washington, D.C.

6. REGISTRATION AGENCY----------------The Bureau of Apprenticeship and
    Training, U.S. Department of
    Labor, Washington, D.C.

7. WORK PROCESS SCHEDULE--------------An outline of work procedures
    which specifies the required
    supervised work experience,
    training on the job, and the
    approximate time to be spent in
    each major process.

8.   SCHEDULE OF RELATED INSTRUCTION --- Organized, related and supple-
mental instruction necessary to
provide apprentices with knowledge in technical subjects
related to the trade. The
instruction may include
supervised correspondence
or self-study courses, as
approved by law or by policy of
the registration agency. A
minimum of 144 hours each year of
apprenticeship training is
required. It may also include
resident instruction at a DOD or
civilian school. Normally,
a minimum of 144 hours annually
is required. However resident,
formal schooling can satisfy
total requirements for related
instruction if over 360 hours are
attained.

WORK PROCESS SCHEDULE FOR THE TRADE
OF AUTOMOTIVE MECHANIC

<u>Job Description</u>. As a result of formal training received in conjunction
with MOS qualification, participants are knowledgeable of the principles
and theories applicable to the various systems that comprise the automotive vehicle, and the construction, principles of operation and functional
interrelationship of components of those systems. They are also qualified
to use the common/special tools, precision measuring instruments and
portable testing equipment associated with the field of automotive repair.
Duties include the performance of first, second, third, and fourth echelon
maintenance on the engines, power transmissions, and brake, steering,
suspension, fuel, and electrical systems employed in military tactical
motor vehicles including 1/4 ton to 10 ton trucks and truck-tractors, and
1/4 ton to 60 ton trailers. Occasionally billet responsibilities may
require the performance of similar functions on standard commercial
vehicles. Specific duties involve the performance of: all inspections,
services, and adjustments associated with routine and scheduled
maintenance of automotive equipment; complete tune-up of fuel electrical
systems; isolating the cause of malfunctions in the various automotive
systems using appropriate diagnostic equipment and following approved
troubleshooting procedures; and effecting the adjustments/repai-
rs/replacements required to correct deficient conditions. Component
repair and overhaul actions are performed on gasoline and diesel engines,
automatic and standard transmissions, differentials, transfers and similar
assemblies/components that reflect standard configuration and are
manufactured by General Motors, Chrysler, Cummins, Continental, American-
Bosch Arma, Delco-Remy, Prestolite, Borg-Warner, and other well known
corporations.

WORK EXPERIENCE FUNCTIONS

Function/Task	Function Hours
A. Vehicle: clean lubricate	345
B. Front End and Steering: inspect adjust aline repair replace	475
C. Rear Axle and Suspension inspect adjust repair replace overhaul	680
D. Brakes Hydraulic: inspect service adjust bleed repair replace overhaul	405
E. Engine: service inspect test troubleshoot repair replace parts overhaul tune	365
F. Cooling System: inspect test service repair replace	320
G. Fuel System (Gasoline): inspect test adjust repair replace overhaul	635

Function/Task	Function Hours
H. Fuel System (Diesel): inspect test adjust calibrate repair replace	755
I. Blower/Turbocharger inspect test repair replace overhaul	400
J. Electrical Systems test troubleshoot repair replace	540
K. Ignition System: inspect adjust time troubleshoot repair replace	390
L. Clutch: inspect adjust repair replace	350
M. Transmission: service test adjust troubleshoot repair replace	515
N. Hydraulic Units service test adjust repair replace	295

Function/Task	Function Hours

O.   Test Equipment:
     test
     maintain
     operate
	220

P.   Special Tools and Machines:
     maintain
     operate
	155

Q.   Miscellaneous:
     supervise
     shop operations
     safety
	155

TOTAL:	8000

NOTE: Accomplishment of specific hours for tasks under each function have not been prescribed on a mandatory basis. Supervisors of apprenticed Marines will endeavor to ensure all tasks are performed in equal proportions in accordance with locally prevailing capabilities.

SCHEDULE OF RELATED INSTRUCTION

Course Number	Course Title	School	Res.	Non Res.	Hours Credit
NA	Basic Automotive Mechanic	MCSSS	X		336
NA	Advanced Automotive Mechanic	MCSSS	X		503
NA	Fuel and Electrical Systems Repair	USAOC&S	X		317
35.8	Automotive Engine Maintenance and Repair	MCI		X	18
35.9	Automotive Power Trains	MCI		X	37
ORD 607	Engine Principles	USAOC&S		X	15
ORD 730	Wheeled Vehicle Maintenance	USAOC&S		X	26
ORD 63B202	Wheeled Vehicle Engines	USAOC&S		X	26
ORD 406	Wheeled Vehicle Engine Maintenance	USAOC&S		X	12
ORD 403	Principles of Fuels and Fuel Systems	USAOC&S		X	16
ORD 727	Electrical Systems and Components	USAOC&S		X	12
ORD 010	Electrical Systems Component Repair	USAOC&S		X	23
ORD 404	Wheeled Vehicle Ignition Systems	USAOC&S		X	28
ORD 405	Wheeled Vehicle Power Train Principles	USAOC&S		X	12
ORD 63B205	Wheeled Vehicle Clutches and Transmissions	USAOC&S		X	22
ORD 63B206	Wheeled Vehicle Drive Lines and Axles	USAOC&S		X	28
ORD 081	Wheeled Vehicle Steering and Suspension	USAOC&S		X	12
ORD 410	Wheeled Vehicle Brake System	USAOC&S		X	15
ORD 417	Hydramatic Transmission	USAOC&S		X	13

Course Number	Course Title	School	Res.	Non Res.	Hours Credit
ORD 531	Mechanical Maintenance of Wheeled and Tracked Vehicles	USAOC&S		X	17
ORD 728	Mechanical Devices and Components	USAOC&S		X	18
ORD 726	Military Vehicles and Engines	USAOC&S		X	15
ORD 098	Fundamentals of Electricity	USAOC&S		X	24
ORD 426	Allied Trades	USAOC&S		X	15

a. A total of 336 hours of formal school and 24 hours of related instruction is required to complete this program.

b. Credit for related instruction from other sources (civilian schools, vocational courses, civilian correspondence courses, etc.) will be evaluated and awarded on a case-by-case basis.

INSTRUCTIONS FOR COMPLETING WORK EXPERIENCE LOG

This pamphlet is issued to each registered apprentice and identifies the occupation, work process training schedules, hours allocated to each training task increment in the work process schedule and supervisory certification requirement.

    1. <u>Marine applicant will</u>:

       a. Complete the apprentice registration application (enclosure 1) in triplicate.

          (1) Submit the application to the commanding officer or his authorized representative.

          (2) Obtain work experience log, which includes the Work Experience Functions. Obtain one year's supply (12 copies) of the Apprentice Work Experience Hourly Record (enclosure 2) from the commanding officer or education officer.

          (3) Have one passport size picture made and complete the (Personal History), enclosure (3).

          (4) Complete (Military Education), enclosure (4), and maintain up to date with certification.

          (5) Complete (Civilian Education), enclosure (5), with certification from the Marine's Service Record Book.

          (6) Maintain (Military Assignment), enclosure (6).

          (7) Civilian Occupation, enclosure (7), if applicable, submit statement to program sponsor on employer letterhead, giving length of employment, position held and manner of performance.

       b. Career oriented apprentice Marines must complete the same requirements as the first-term apprentice except that they will be given credit for one-half the hours required for the specific program in which they are enrolled. This is provided their previous enlistment was served in an MOS applicable to the relevant apprenticeship program for which they are applying.

(1) A photocopy of Military Assignment, enclosure (6) of the work log with certification will be forwarded to MOS sponsor.

COMMANDING OFFICER
MOTOR TRANSPORT SCHOOL COMPANY
MARINE CORPS SERVICE SUPPORT SCHOOLS
MARINE CORPS BASE
CAMP LEJEUNE, NORTH CAROLINA   28542

(2) The program sponsor will then assign credit hours in accordance with MCO 1550.22 and return to the applicant's commanding officer.

2. <u>Procedures for recording hourly work experience</u>

a. Daily Record: Daily entries will be made by the apprentice.

b. Weekly certification by supervisor: Weekly certification will be completed by the shop chief for whom the Marine works.

c. Consolidation/Certification on Month/Yearly recapitulation: The signature line of the work experience hourly report will be signed by the commanding officer or his representative. This report will reflect the entries for the monthly work experience, enclosure (8) of work experience log.

3. <u>Semiannual progress interview</u>

a. Report to Education Officer within 5 to 8 months after date of this application and twice a year thereafter. Enclosure (9) will be completed and forwarded to CMC (Code OTTE).

b. The purpose of the interview is to determine the status of the apprentice and certify a photocopy of the last hourly record of work experience.

c. The Commanding Officer or Education Officer/ authorized representative will sign the Apprentice Progress! Status Report (enclosure (9)).

4. <u>Interruption of Assignment</u>

a. Rifle Range leave. Record on the experience hourly report the days away from regular assigned duty.

b. Separation from Active Duty. Status report will be submitted to CMC identifying the Marine as being discharged. Upon request, CMC will forward the records to Bureau of Apprenticeship and Training in the Marine's home state of record

       C. Sickness and hospitalization. Recorded by day on the Apprentice Work Hourly Report.

       d. Voluntary Disenrollment. An apprentice must request suspension or cancellation. Suspension retains the apprentice in a temporary status for no more than one year. A request for suspension may be mailed directly to CMC (Code OTTE) via the chain of command by the apprentice. Cancellation removes the apprentice from the apprenticeship program. A request for cancellation requires the signature of the apprentice's Commanding Officer or Education Officer.

5. <u>Documentation Required to Validate Related Instruction</u>. Certification of completion or transcript of grades will be used to award credit hours toward completion of the apprenticeship program

6. <u>Loss of Work Experience Log</u>

       a. Request a reissue of a blank log from the Education Officer of your command.

       b. Request CMC to furnish data available in your records to bring the log up to date.

APPRENTICE REGISTRATION APPLICATION (1500)
NAVMC 11013 (3-77)
SN: 0000-00-004-6600 U/I: SH

1. Print or type.
2. Prepare in triplicate.
3. Forward original and one copy to CMC (Code OTTE).
4. Apprentice retains one copy in Work Experience Log.

PRIVACY ACT NOTIFICATION

Under the authority of Title 5, U.S. Code, Section 301, the information regarding your former and present active military service, educational background and present personal data is requested in order to review and evaluate your qualifications for the Department of Labor apprenticeship program for active-duty Marine Corps personnel. Your Social Security Number is used for purposes of individual identification. This information will be retained by the Commandant of the Marine Corps (Code OTTE) and by the Bureau of Apprenticeship and Training, U.S. Department of Labor, and will not be divulged without your written authorization to anyone other than Headquarters Marine Corps and Department of Labor personnel involved with administration of this program. You are not required to provide this information, however, failure to do so may result in your not being registered for an apprenticeable trade.

APPLICANT INFORMATION

1. NAME (Last, first, middle)	2. SSN	3. DATE OF BIRTH (Day, Month, Year)	4. SEX ☐ MALE ☐ FEMALE

5. RACE/ETHNIC GROUP
☐ CAUCASIAN/WHITE ☐ NEGRO/BLACK ☐ AMERICAN INDIAN ☐ SPANISH AMERICAN ☑ ORIENTAL ☐ INFORMATION NOT AVAILABLE ☐ NOT ELSEWHERE CLASSIFIED

6. NAME AND LOCATION OF HIGH SCHOOL FROM WHICH GRADUATED	OR, STATE AND DATE OF GED EQUIVALENCY

7. Did you serve on active duty on or after 5 August 1964 and before 9 May 1975? ☐ YES ☐ NO	8. HOME OF RECORD (State)

9. APPRENTICEABLE TRADE FOR REGISTRATION (Give complete title)	10. DOT CODE FOR APPRENTICEABLE TRADE	11. APPRENTICE PROGRAM

I agree to report to the education officer within 6 to 8 months after date of this application and twice a year thereafter. I understand that my registration is voluntary and that registration does not guarantee work or duty assignments appropriate to my apprenticeship. I have read and understand the Privacy Act Statement.

12. Signature of applicant	13. Date

TO BE FILLED IN BY APPLICANT'S COMMANDING OFFICER OR EDUCATION OFFICER

TO: Commandant of the Marine Corps (Code OTTE), Headquarters U.S. Marine Corps, Washington, D.C. 20380

14. FROM

15. Total hours required for term of apprenticeship _____ hours

16. Hours credit given for previous work experience (-) _____ hours

17. Total hours remaining for term of apprenticeship _____ hours

18. COMMENTS (If any)

19. SIGNATURE OF REGISTRAR The applicant has been counseled as to the conditions and requirements of the apprenticeship. Signature _____	20. TITLE	21. DATE

INSTRUCTIONS FOR APPRENTICE REGISTRATION APPLICATION

1. Self-explanatory.

2. Enter Social Security Number. Example: 399-03-6433

3. Enter date of birth: Day, Month, Year.

4. Self-explanatory.

5. Self-explanatory

6. Self-explanatory.

7. A check "X" in the YES block signifies that the registrant is regarded as a Viet Name veteran by the Department of Labor.

8. Enter name of state which the registrant calls home.

9. Enter long title of apprenticeable trade. Example: Camera Repairer. Entries are limited to those apprenticeships authorized by the Commandant of the Marine Corps.

10. Enter 9-digit DOT code which matches the apprenticeable trade entered in Item 9. The Work Processes Schedule indicates this code.

11. No entry required.

12. Self-explanatory.

13. Self-explanatory.

14. Enter name and address of command forwarding application.

15. Enter total term of the apprenticeship (required hours for completion). Example: 6000. The Work Processes Schedule indicates the total term of the apprenticeship.

16. Enter hours of creditable work experience completed prior to registration, if any. A registrant may be credited with 1000 hours of previous work experience for each full year that his/her service record validates assignment to an MOS applicable to the apprenticeable trade. Applicable MOSs, if any, are listed at the bottom of the Work Processes Schedule for each authorized apprenticeable trade. However, credit for previous work experience completed prior to registration cannot exceed more than 50% of the term of the apprenticeship. Therefore, no more than 3000 hours of previous work experience can be credited to a 6000-hour apprenticeship. Portions or fractions of years of work experience will not be credited.

17. Enter the difference between Item 15 and Item 16. This difference is the number of work experience hours which must be completed by the apprentice.

18. Enter any comments regarding previous work experience, future assignment or next duty, or further explanation of any above item. Entry not mandatory.

19. Signature of commanding officer, education officer, or his authorized representative.

20. Title of registrar who signed Item 19.

21. Enter date that Item 19 was signed. This will be the effective beginning date of the apprenticeship.

(AUTOMOTIVE MECHANIC MOS 3521/3522)

APPRENTICE WORK EXPERIENCE HOURLY REPORT (NAVMC 11015)

_____
NAME (Last, First, Middle)

1. Print legibly.
2. Enter completed hours daily or weekly.
3. Have supervisor verify hours at the end of each week.
4. Keep this record in your Work Experience Log.

Week of	Date From		Date To						Signature & Title of Supervisor							
Day	A	B	C	D	E	F	G	H	I	J	K	L	M	N	O	P	Q	Total Hours
Sun																		
Mon																		
Tues																		
Wed																		
Thur																		
Fri																		
Sat																		
Total Hours																		

Week of	Date From		Date To						Signature & Title of Supervisor							
Day	A	B	C	D	E	F	G	H	I	J	K	L	M	N	O	P	Q	Total Hours
Sun																		
Mon																		
Tues																		
Wed																		
Thur																		
Fri																		
Sat																		
Total Hours																		

A. Vehicle
B. Front End and Steering
C. Rear Axle and Suspension
O. Brakes Hydraulic
E. Engine
F. Cooling System
G. Fuel System (Gasoline)
H. Fuel System (Diesel)
I. Blower/Turbocharger
J. Electrical Systems
K. Ignition System
L. Clutch
M. Transmission
N. Hydraulic Units
O. Test Equipment
P. Special Tools and Machines
Q. Miscellaneous

Enclosure (2)

SIGNATURE & TITLE   DATE

Enclosure (2)

PERSONAL HISTORY

LAST NAME	FIRST NAME	MI

RANK	SOCIAL SECURITY NUMBER	DATE OF BIRTH DAY, MONTH, YEAR

PLACE OF BIRTH - ADDRESS

HOME OF RECORD - ADDRESS

ATTACH PASSPORT SIZE
PHOTO IN THE SPACE

SIGNATURE OF APPRENTICE	DATE

MILITARY EDUCATION

COURSE TITLE	LOCATION	LENGTH FR:	TO:
Basic Automotive Mechanic Course			
Advanced Automotive Mechanic Course			
Other Related Courses:			

Total Education Hrs:	1st Year Hrs:	Certified	2nd Year Hrs:	Certified	3rd Year Hrs:	Certified

CIVILIAN EDUCATION

HIGH SCHOOL OR GED	NAME, ADDRESS, ZIP CODE	DATE GRADUATED

COLLEGE OR GED	NAME, ADDRESS, ZIP CODE	DATE GRADUATED

VOCATIONAL SCHOOLS

LIST ALL SEPARATE COURSES TAKEN

LIST ALL OTHER SPECIALIZED TRAINING NOT COVERED ABOVE

MILITARY ASSIGNMENT

UNIT	ADDRESS	FROM	TO	DUTY ASSIGNMENT

CIVILIAN OCCUPATION

LIST ALL MOTOR TRANSPORT RELATED CIVILIAN EMPLOYMENT COVERING LAST 10 YEARS		
FIRM - NAME AND ADDRESS	NO. YEARS	POSITION HELD

WORK EXPERIENCE FOR _____
(YEAR)

	Jan	Feb	Mar	Apr	May	Jun	Jul	Aug	Sep	Oct	Nov	Dec	Total For Yr	Int
A														
B														
C														
D														
E														
F														
G														
H														
I														
J														
K														
L														
M														
N														
O														
P														
Q														
INT														

A.	Vehicle	J.	Electrical Systems
B.	Front End and Steering	K.	Ignition Systems
C.	Rear Axle and Suspension	L.	Clutch
O.	Brakes Hydraulic	M.	Transmission
E.	Engine	N.	Hydraulic Units
F.	Cooling System	O.	Test Equipment
G.	Fuel System (Gasoline)	P.	Special Tools and Machines
H.	Fuel System (Diesel)	Q.	Miscellaneous
I.	Blower/Turbocharger		

_____

CERTIFlCATION OFFICIAL

_____

TITLE

Enclosure (8)

APPRENTICE PROGRESS/STATUS REPORT (1500)

NAVMC 11014 (3-77)

SN: 0000-00-008-6820 U/I: SH

1. Print or type.
2. Prepare in triplicate.
3. Forward original and one copy to CMC (Code OTTE) with attached photo of last Hourly Record of Work Experience.
4. Apprentice retains one copy in Work Experience Log.

PRIVACY ACT NOTIFICATION

Under the authority of Title S, U.S. Code, Section 301, the information regarding your former and present military service, educational background and present personal data is requested for purposes of individual identification. This information will be retained by the Commandant of the Marine Corps (Code OTTE) and by the Bureau of Apprenticeship and Training, U.S. Department of Labor and will not be divulged without your written authorization to anyone other than Headquarters Marine Corps and Department of Labor personnel involved with the administration of the apprenticeship program. You are not required to provide this information; however, failure to do so may result in cancellation of your registration in an apprenticeable trade.

To be filled in by Apprentice or official in accordance with instructions on reverse side.

1. NAME OF APPRENTICE (Last, first, middle)	2. SSN	3. SEX ☐ MALE ☐ FEMALE

4. RACE/ETHNIC GROUP
☐ CAUCASIAN/ WHITE ☐ NEGRO/ BLACK ☐ AMERICAN INDIAN ☐ SPANISH AMERICAN ☐ ORIENTAL ☐ INFORMATION NOT AVAILABLE ☐ NOT ELSEWHERE CLASSIFIED

5. Did you serve on active duty on or after 5 August 1964 and before 8 May 1975? ☐ YES ☐ NO

6. HOME OF RECORD (State)

7. Apprenticeable Trade in Which Registered	8. Total Hours for Term	9. Hrs. Preregistration Experience	10. Hrs. Completed Since Registration	11. Hours Remaining

TO: Commandant of the Marine Corps (Code OTTE), Headquarters U.S. Marine Corps, Washington, D.C. 20380

12. FROM (Activity submitting report)

ACTION REQUESTED

(check one)

13. Please suspend registration for the apprentice named above for the reason(s) checked below:

a. ☐ Orders to light duty

b. ☐ Nature of current assignment prohibits work in apprenticeable trade for one year or less

c. ☐ Hospitalization

d. ☐ Operational commitments prevent reporting for progress interview

14. ☐ Please lift the suspension of registration for the apprentice named above effective: _____
(Date)

15. ☐ Please cancel the registration of the apprentice named above for the reason(s) checked below:

a. ☐ Commanding officer's prerogative

b. ☐ Discharge or release to inactive duty

c. ☐ Termination of work experience for one year or more

d. ☐ Death

e. ☐ Failure to report for twice-a-year apprentice progress interview

f. ☐ Personal request of apprentice

16. ☐ The apprentice named above has completed all required hours of work experience in all areas of the apprentice trade. A "Certificate of Apprenticeship Completion" is requested.

17. SIGNATURE OF APPRENTICE	18. DATE

19. SIGNATURE AND TITLE OF OFFICIAL	20. DATE

INSTRUCTIONS FOR APPRENTICE PROGRESS/STATUS REPORT

Item No.

1. Self-explanatory.
2. Enter Social Security Number. Example: 399-03-8433.
3. Self-explanatory.
4. Self-explanatory. Must agree with Item 5 of apprentice registration.
5. Entry must agree with Item 7 of apprentice registration.
6. Enter name of state which the apprentice calls home.
7. Enter long title of apprenticeable trade. Example: Camera Repairer.

ITEMS 8, 9, 10, and 11 NOT REQUIRED IF SUSPENSION (Item 13) OR CANCELLATION (Item 15) 15 REQUESTED.

8. Enter total term of apprenticeship as indicated on Work Processes Schedule. Must agree with Item 15 of "Apprentice Registration application."

9. Enter number of verified hours of work experience completed prior to registration. Must agree with Item 16 of "Apprentice Registration Application.

10. Enter cumulative number of hours of work experience completed as a registered apprentice. Attach reproduced copy (photostat or xerox) of every "Work Experience Hourly Record" which shows hours completed since last report

11. Add Item 9 and Item 10 and subtract total from Item 8. Enter result in Item 11.

12. Name and address of activity from which report is submitted.

13. Check if this is a request for suspension. Suspension retains the apprentice in a temporary inactive status for no more than one year. Request for suspension requires signature of apprentice in Item 17. A request for a suspension may be mailed directly to Commandant of the Marine Corps by apprentice. No suspension will be carried longer than one year.

14. Check here if reason for suspension no longer applies. A request for lifting suspension requires signature of apprentice in Item 17 and signature of Commanding Officer or Education Officer in tern 19.

15. Check here is this is a request for cancellation. Cancellation removes the apprentice from the apprenticeship program. A request for cancellation requires signature of Commanding Officer or Education Officer in Item 19.

16. Check if apprentice has completed all required work experience, both grand total of hours and total hours in each skill area. A check in this block must be supported by final entries in Items 8, 9, 10 and 11, plus a produced copy of the "Work Experience Hourly Record" completed since the last apprentice progress interview or report. Hours of verified work experience completed before registration (Item 9), if any, will be distributed equally among the skill area of the trade. A check in this block requires signatures in Item 17 and Item 19.

17. Signature of apprentice required for Items 8, 9, 10, 11, 13, 14, 1Sf and 16.

18. Date in which signature of apprentice is affixed in Item 1 7.

19. Signature of commanding officer or education officer submitting report required for Items 8, 9, 10, 11, 13, 14, 15a and 15f.

20. Date on which signature in Item 19 is affixed.

Certificate of Completion of Apprenticeship

United States Department of Labor

Bureau of Apprenticeship and Training

This is to certify that

has completed an apprenticeship in the trade of

in accordance with the standards recommended by the
Federal Committee on Apprenticeship

SAMPLE

DEPARTMENT OF LABOR · UNITED STATES OF AMERICA

DATE COMPLETED

SECRETARY OF LABOR

William H. Kolberg
ASSISTANT SECRETARY FOR MANPOWER

Hugh C. Murphy
BUREAU ADMINISTRATOR

29